Dark Web Syndicate:

The Cybercrime

Empire

The Secret Economy of Crime—How AlphaBay
Built the Largest Illegal Marketplace in Internet
History and the Rise & Fall of a Billion-Dollar Black
Market

By

Jack Michael

Jack Michael

DEDICATION

This book is dedicated to those who tirelessly fight against cybercrime—the investigators, cybersecurity experts, and journalists who work behind the scenes to expose digital criminals. To the victims of online fraud, identity theft, and the dark web's illicit trade, your stories matter. To the readers who seek knowledge beyond the surface of the internet, may this book open your eyes to the hidden world shaping our digital future. The pursuit of truth is never-ending, and awareness is the first step toward justice.

ACKNOWLEDGMENTS

This book would not have been possible without the dedication of those who have spent years researching the complexities of cybercrime and the dark web. I extend my gratitude to cybersecurity professionals, law enforcement officials, investigative journalists, and digital forensics experts whose work inspired this project. Special thanks to my readers—your curiosity and engagement fuel the exploration of these hidden realities. To those working to secure the internet, your efforts shape the future of digital safety.

Jack Michael

TABLE OF CONTENTS

INTRODUCTION

There exists a world beneath the surface of what we know—a hidden economy fueled by anonymity, encrypted transactions, and the darkest desires of human nature. It is a place where identities vanish into strings of random characters, fortunes are amassed in currencies that leave no trace, and the trade of illicit goods flows as freely as water. Here, a single click can secure a new identity, order a lethal weapon, or purchase narcotics so pure they rival the production labs of the world's most powerful cartels. This is the dark web, the shadowy underbelly of the internet, where crime is not just committed—it is systemized, industrialized, and scaled to an unfathomable degree.

In the heart of this clandestine empire stood AlphaBay, the largest and most sophisticated black market in digital history. Unlike its predecessors, it wasn't merely an underground forum for petty criminals. It was a fully operational e-commerce empire, indistinguishable from legal platforms like Amazon or eBay—except that everything it offered was illegal. Drugs, counterfeit documents, hacking tools, stolen data, weapons—if it could be sold, AlphaBay had a marketplace for it. But what made it truly extraordinary wasn't just the sheer volume of its transactions; it was the level of professionalism with which it was run. Vendors had ratings. Buyers left reviews. Refund policies and dispute resolutions were in place. And all of it was wrapped in layers of encryption so deep that even the most advanced law enforcement agencies in the world struggled to break through.

At the helm of this digital empire was a man whose name, at first, meant nothing to the world. He was neither a cartel kingpin nor a hardened criminal mastermind lurking in the shadows. Instead, he was an unassuming figure—a tech-savvy entrepreneur whose empire was built not with brute force, but with lines of code. Alexandre Cazes, known online as Alpha02, did not rely on violence or intimidation. He didn't need to. His power came from his ability to outmaneuver, to remain invisible, to manipulate the very fabric of cyberspace itself. He wasn't just running a marketplace; he was redefining the way crime operated in the digital age.

For years, AlphaBay thrived, seemingly untouchable. Law enforcement agencies across the globe watched in frustration as its user base exploded, its revenues soared into the billions, and its operators remained ghosts in the machine. They knew it had to be stopped, but taking it down was another matter entirely. This was not a street-level operation. This was not a lone hacker making careless mistakes. AlphaBay was fortified with some of the most advanced security measures ever seen in the criminal underworld. Yet, despite its digital walls, its untraceable transactions, and its army of anonymous users, its downfall was not the result of cutting-edge law enforcement tactics. It was not taken down by a sophisticated cyber operation. Instead, it crumbled because of something far more human—a small, seemingly insignificant mistake, the kind that even the most careful criminals make when they start believing in their own invincibility.

What followed was one of the most ambitious cybercrime takedowns in history—a global effort that spanned multiple countries, law enforcement agencies, and intelligence operations. It was a high-stakes cat-and-mouse game where the line between hunter and hunted blurred with every passing moment. And at the center of it all was a man who thought he had outsmarted the system, only to find himself trapped in the very web he had woven.

This is the story of AlphaBay. A story of genius and greed, of power and paranoia, of the rise of a digital empire and the small misstep that brought it all crashing down. It is a tale that unfolds in the shadows, where criminals trade in whispers and fortunes are made in the dead of night. It is a reminder that no matter how well-hidden a secret may be, the truth has a way of surfacing. And in the world of cybercrime, the difference between invincibility and vulnerability is often just a single, overlooked detail.

Turn the page. The world you think you know is about to change.

CHAPTER 1

Enter the Dark Web

There is an entire world beneath the internet that most people use every day. A hidden network of encrypted websites, invisible to search engines, inaccessible through standard browsers, and operating beyond the reach of traditional law enforcement. It is a place where anonymity is absolute, where transactions leave no paper trail, and where identities dissolve into meaningless strings of numbers and letters. It is known as the dark web, and within its depths, an entire underground economy thrives—a marketplace where anything can be bought or sold, and where the line between reality and digital fiction blurs into something unrecognizable.

Unlike the internet most people are familiar with—the one filled with social media platforms, news websites, and online shopping—the dark web is not designed for casual browsing. It exists within the deep web, the portion of the internet that isn't indexed by search engines, where databases, academic journals, medical records, and private emails reside. But while the deep web consists mostly of benign, restricted-access content, the dark web is something else entirely. It is a hidden ecosystem intentionally shrouded in secrecy, a network of unlisted websites that can only be accessed through specialized tools. The surface web—the part of the internet where most people operate—is like a city filled with clearly marked roads and buildings, with street signs pointing the way. The dark web, however, is more like an uncharted wilderness, where every path leads somewhere unknown, and every encounter carries a degree of uncertainty.

At the heart of the dark web is Tor, an open-source anonymity network originally developed by the U.S. Naval Research Laboratory for secure communications. Tor, short for The Onion Router, functions by bouncing internet traffic through a series of randomly selected relay nodes around the world, effectively obscuring a user's location and identity. When a person connects to the dark web through Tor, their internet activity is rerouted multiple times across encrypted servers, making it nearly impossible to trace their origin. This technology, initially designed to protect government intelligence and dissidents in oppressive regimes, quickly found another use—one that was never intended. Criminals, hackers, and illicit traders saw in Tor the perfect tool to conduct illegal business beyond the reach of authorities.

Accessing the dark web is as simple as downloading the Tor browser, a modified version of Firefox designed to navigate .onion websites—domains that function outside of conventional internet protocols. Unlike .com, .org, or .net websites, .onion addresses are randomly generated strings of characters that provide no indication of what lies within. Clicking on one could lead to a political forum for whistleblowers, an underground drug marketplace, or an empty shell designed to lure unsuspecting users into a trap. Because of its anonymity, the dark web serves both noble and nefarious purposes. It is used by journalists, activists, and political dissidents in oppressive countries to bypass censorship and communicate securely. But it is also used by cybercriminals to traffic in stolen data, counterfeit documents, illegal drugs, and even more disturbing enterprises.

The foundation of illegal trade on the dark web was built long before AlphaBay came into existence. In the early 2010s, a marketplace called Silk Road revolutionized the way contraband was bought and sold online. Modeled after e-commerce giants like eBay and Amazon, Silk Road offered a sophisticated platform where users could browse listings, communicate with sellers, and purchase illegal goods using cryptocurrency. It was the first real dark web marketplace to gain global attention, and its impact was profound. Law enforcement agencies scrambled to shut it down, recognizing that traditional methods of crime-fighting were ineffective in a world where transactions were anonymous, and buyers and sellers never had to meet in person.

Silk Road's eventual takedown in 2013 was a warning shot, but it was not the end of dark web marketplaces. On the contrary, it was only the beginning. The site's success proved that there was enormous demand for a secure, anonymous marketplace where illegal goods could be exchanged freely. In the years that followed, dozens of new markets emerged, each improving on the last. With each takedown, another would rise in its place, stronger and more resilient. And then came AlphaBay—the most powerful, sophisticated, and ambitious dark web marketplace the world had ever seen.

What made the dark web so appealing to criminals was not just its anonymity but the fact that it removed many of the risks associated with traditional illicit trade. A street-level drug dealer, for example, faced constant dangers—law enforcement, violent competitors, unreliable suppliers. But on the dark web, those risks were minimized. Buyers and sellers never met face-to-face. They never exchanged real names. Transactions were completed through encrypted messaging and blockchain-based cryptocurrencies that, in theory, left no trace. The dark web took the illicit economy and transformed it into something streamlined, efficient, and scalable on a global level.

The world of cybercrime was evolving, and with it, so were the criminals. The early pioneers of dark web marketplaces had been digital anarchists, people who believed in the right to free trade beyond government control. But as the dark web matured, ideology gave way to pure capitalism. AlphaBay was not about philosophy or rebellion—it was about money. Its founder was not some radical libertarian trying to upend the system. He was a businessman. And his business would change the world of cybercrime forever.

CHAPTER 2

The Birth of AlphaBay

There was nothing remarkable about Alexandre Cazes at first glance. He wasn't a cartel boss, a hardened criminal, or someone who had spent years in the underworld refining his craft. He was, by all accounts, an ordinary man with an extraordinary understanding of technology. Born in Canada, Cazes was a self-taught programmer, someone who had grown up surrounded by computers, dissecting their inner workings, learning how systems functioned— and, more importantly, how they could be manipulated. His fascination with coding was not just a skill; it was an obsession. Long before he became the mastermind behind the world's most notorious dark web marketplace, he was already making a name for himself in hacker circles.

Cazes had a natural ability to see the gaps in cybersecurity, the weak points that most people overlooked. He began by selling hacking tools and stolen credentials online, carving out a small niche for himself in underground forums where digital criminals traded knowledge. He was ambitious, resourceful, and, above all, relentless in his pursuit of financial success. As he moved deeper into the world of cybercrime, he realized something crucial—while hackers were skilled at breaching security systems, the real money wasn't in the act of hacking itself. The true wealth was in providing a marketplace where others could conduct illegal business securely.

By the time Silk Road collapsed in 2013, Cazes saw an opportunity. He had watched as law enforcement took down dark web markets one by one, but he also understood why they had failed. Their security flaws, their operational missteps—these were lessons that could be learned from, weaknesses that could be reinforced. He was ready to build something better, something stronger. And in 2014, AlphaBay was born.

Unlike its predecessors, AlphaBay was not a hastily thrown-together marketplace riddled with vulnerabilities. It was a polished, professional platform, designed with the efficiency of a Silicon Valley startup but operating entirely outside the law. Its interface mimicked mainstream e-commerce sites, making it familiar to users accustomed to platforms like eBay and Amazon. It had search filters, product categories, and detailed descriptions. Users could browse with ease, compare vendors, read customer reviews, and leave feedback on their purchases. The goal was simple—to make the process of buying illegal goods as smooth and convenient as shopping for household items online.

The market structure of AlphaBay was unlike anything seen before. While Silk Road had primarily focused on narcotics, AlphaBay expanded its offerings into nearly every conceivable category of illicit trade. It was not just a drug marketplace—it was a hub for digital fraud, counterfeit documents, firearms, hacking tools, and stolen financial data. A person could buy a fake passport, access hacked bank accounts, purchase malware to infiltrate secure networks, and even hire a cybercriminal for specialized services. Anything that could be sold, AlphaBay had a vendor for it.

One of its most revolutionary features was the implementation of an escrow system, which provided a layer of security for both buyers and sellers. Instead of transactions occurring directly between parties, AlphaBay held funds in a temporary account until both sides confirmed that the deal was complete. This eliminated scams and ensured that users felt confident in their purchases. Disputes were handled through a professional resolution system, where moderators acted as arbitrators, much like in legitimate online marketplaces.

But perhaps the most critical element of AlphaBay's success was its payment system. It relied entirely on cryptocurrency, primarily Bitcoin and Monero. While Bitcoin had been the standard for dark web transactions, it still left traces that skilled forensic analysts could follow. Monero, on the other hand, was built for absolute anonymity. Its blockchain was designed in such a way that transactions were virtually untraceable, making it the perfect currency for criminals who wanted to operate beyond the reach of law enforcement.

As AlphaBay grew, so did its reputation. Vendors flocked to the platform, eager to sell their products in an environment that offered unparalleled security and access to a massive customer base. Buyers felt comfortable knowing that they were dealing with vetted sellers, protected by an escrow system, and able to purchase items without fear of being scammed. Law enforcement agencies watched in frustration as the site flourished, knowing that it had taken the best elements of previous dark web markets and refined them into something nearly impenetrable.

What set AlphaBay apart from Silk Road, Evolution, and other defunct marketplaces was not just its scale but its adaptability. Cazes ran it like a business, not a criminal operation. He constantly updated its security features, introduced new payment methods, and even implemented customer service mechanisms to enhance the user experience. Unlike Silk Road, which had been run by a man with ideological motivations, AlphaBay was purely about profit. There was no political stance, no manifesto about government overreach—only the cold, calculated efficiency of a black-market empire built for maximum financial gain.

The numbers spoke for themselves. At its peak, AlphaBay was processing an estimated **$600,000 to $800,000 in transactions daily**, making it the most profitable black market ever seen on the dark web. It had tens of thousands of vendors, hundreds of thousands of customers, and an infrastructure designed to withstand scrutiny. But as powerful as it had become, as secure as it seemed, there was one thing Cazes had overlooked—himself.

For all his precautions, for all his meticulous planning, AlphaBay's greatest vulnerability was not in its code or its servers. It was in the man who had built it. And like so many before him, it was only a matter of time before that vulnerability was exposed.

CHAPTER 3

The Billion-Dollar Marketplace

In the hidden corridors of the internet, AlphaBay thrived as the most sophisticated and profitable dark web marketplace ever created. Unlike the crude forums and scattered black-market sites that had come before it, AlphaBay operated with the smooth efficiency of a high-end e-commerce platform. It had become an underground giant, facilitating billions of dollars in illegal transactions, all while its users remained cloaked in anonymity. Its vast marketplace catered to every illicit demand imaginable, transforming the way criminals did business in the digital age.

What made AlphaBay so powerful was its sheer range of offerings. It was not a marketplace with a singular focus, like Silk Road, which had been largely dedicated to the sale of narcotics. Instead, AlphaBay was a one-stop-shop for all things illegal, a digital empire where criminals, fraudsters, and cyber-mercenaries could conduct business with a level of convenience that had never been seen before.

A significant portion of AlphaBay's trade revolved around fake documentation. With just a few clicks, a buyer could secure an authentic-looking passport from virtually any country, complete with biometric data and official stamps. High-quality driver's licenses, diplomas, and birth certificates were readily available, allowing criminals to forge new identities or legitimize their scams. These documents were used for everything from financial fraud to human trafficking, creating a hidden economy of synthetic identities that made it difficult for law enforcement to track criminals across borders.

But for many, AlphaBay's primary attraction was its extensive selection of narcotics. Cocaine, heroin, methamphetamine, ecstasy, LSD—every imaginable drug was available, often with detailed descriptions and purity guarantees. Vendors marketed their products much like legitimate businesses, offering lab-tested assurances, customer reviews, and stealth packaging to evade detection. Buyers no longer had to risk face-to-face transactions with street dealers. Instead, they could browse through pages of product listings, compare suppliers, and have their orders discreetly shipped to their doorstep, often concealed within seemingly ordinary items like books, DVDs, or vacuum-sealed food packaging.

Weapons were another major component of AlphaBay's economy. While mainstream gun laws restricted access to firearms in many parts of the world, AlphaBay had no such limitations. Handguns, semi-automatic rifles, and even military-grade weapons were sold to buyers willing to pay the right price. These weapons were often sourced from conflict zones, stolen armories, or illicit manufacturers operating outside regulatory oversight. Buyers seeking even more lethal means had access to unregistered firearms—so-called "ghost guns"—that could be assembled with little expertise.

Beyond drugs and firearms, AlphaBay's digital black market was a hub for financial crime. Stolen credit card data, online banking credentials, and hacked PayPal accounts were available in abundance. Cybercriminals could purchase full identity kits— known as "fullz"—which contained everything needed to commit large-scale fraud, including names, addresses, social security numbers, and even bank login details. Hacking tools and malware were openly traded, allowing even those with minimal technical expertise to exploit security vulnerabilities, breach corporate networks, and steal sensitive data.

The darkest corners of AlphaBay extended beyond financial fraud and illegal goods. The marketplace had sections for more insidious services—hired cyber-mercenaries offering hacking-for-hire, blackmail services, and, in the most extreme cases, alleged contract killers. While many of these so-called "hitman" listings were likely scams designed to prey on desperate criminals, their very existence fueled the perception that AlphaBay had no ethical boundaries. If there was demand, there was supply. The marketplace operated on a principle of pure capitalism, with no moral constraints to limit what could be bought or sold.

What made AlphaBay's empire truly unstoppable—at least for a time—was its reliance on cryptocurrency. Traditional banking systems were useless in an economy where both buyers and sellers needed to remain anonymous. Credit card payments and bank transfers left a trail, one that law enforcement could follow. But Bitcoin and Monero changed the game.

These decentralized currencies allowed users to transfer funds without intermediaries, without banks, and without direct ties to their real-world identities.

Bitcoin was the standard currency for dark web transactions, but it was not perfect. Its blockchain, while anonymous in many respects, was still public. Skilled forensic analysts could track transactions if they were linked to real-world activities, leading to potential exposure. This limitation led to the rise of Monero, a privacy-focused cryptocurrency designed specifically to obscure transaction details. Unlike Bitcoin, Monero's ledger did not publicly display wallet addresses or transaction amounts, making it nearly impossible to trace funds. For criminals operating on AlphaBay, it was the perfect financial tool—money that existed without oversight, free from the prying eyes of governments and law enforcement.

Once an order was placed on AlphaBay, a complex logistics network ensured that products reached buyers while minimizing the risk of interception. Vendors employed creative concealment tactics, using everyday items to disguise contraband. Drugs were hidden inside common household objects—cosmetic containers, DVD cases, even greeting cards. Some sellers vacuum-sealed products inside food packaging, making them appear completely normal during routine customs inspections. In some cases, illicit goods were concealed inside children's toys or electronic devices, further reducing suspicion.

Shipping routes were carefully planned to avoid detection. Many vendors relied on a technique known as "dead drops," where a buyer would receive a set of GPS coordinates rather than a direct shipment, allowing them to retrieve their package from a public location rather than their home address. In some cases, criminals took advantage of loopholes in international shipping regulations, routing packages through multiple countries to obscure their origin. Postal services, overwhelmed with millions of packages daily, had little ability to detect these hidden transactions.

For years, this system worked flawlessly. Vendors continued to profit, customers received their illicit goods without consequence, and AlphaBay took its cut from every transaction. It was a digital empire unlike anything the criminal world had seen before— an unstoppable machine fueled by greed, innovation, and the sheer anonymity of the internet.

But no empire, no matter how carefully built, is indestructible. The very things that made AlphaBay untouchable—its sophisticated security, its reliance on cryptocurrency, its sprawling marketplace—would eventually become the cracks through which law enforcement would find its way inside. And as it turned out, the biggest flaw in the system was not in the technology, but in the man who had built it.

CHAPTER 4

AlphaBay's Growth and Global Impact

From the moment it launched, AlphaBay grew at an unprecedented pace, quickly establishing itself as the dominant force in the underground economy. It began as a modest marketplace, attracting small-time vendors and buyers who had once relied on Silk Road and other now-defunct dark web platforms. But within a matter of months, it had expanded into something far larger—an empire that spanned continents, powered by the seamless fusion of anonymity, cryptocurrency, and the insatiable demand for illicit goods.

The platform's rapid ascent was no accident. AlphaBay was designed for scale, built to accommodate thousands of vendors and hundreds of thousands of customers without collapsing under its own weight. While early dark web markets had struggled with security breaches, poor infrastructure, and unreliable payment systems, AlphaBay refined every aspect of the experience. It was not just a place to buy illegal goods; it was a **well-oiled machine**, a business model perfected for the underground economy.

With every transaction, AlphaBay's influence grew. Criminal syndicates, cyber-fraud groups, and drug cartels recognized its potential and **moved their operations online**, using the platform to expand their reach beyond physical borders. Where traditional organized crime was limited by location and physical interactions, AlphaBay provided something far more lucrative—access to a **global marketplace** where transactions could be carried out in absolute secrecy.

Vendors from Russia, North America, Europe, and Asia flooded the platform, offering everything from high-purity heroin sourced from Southeast Asia to premium counterfeit credit cards freshly stolen from hacked databases. It wasn't just low-level criminals making deals anymore. **Major cybercrime syndicates** began using AlphaBay as a distribution hub, utilizing its escrow system to move millions of dollars' worth of illicit goods every month. Unlike street-level operations that required risky hand-to-hand exchanges, AlphaBay allowed them to conduct business at scale, minimizing exposure while maximizing profit.

As the marketplace expanded, so did its reputation. It became known as the **"Amazon of the Dark Web"**—a title that was both fitting and deeply unsettling. Just as Amazon had revolutionized online shopping with its seamless interface and customer-centric approach, AlphaBay did the same for the illicit economy. Vendors competed for positive reviews, ensuring high-quality products and reliable delivery. Customers had access to thousands of listings, all categorized and filtered for easy browsing. The user experience was so refined that even those who had never engaged in illegal activities before found themselves tempted by the ease of access.

The numbers were staggering. At its peak, AlphaBay had over **400,000 users**, with daily transactions surpassing **$600,000 to $800,000**, amounting to over **$1 billion in total revenue**. It outpaced every other dark web market in history, leaving authorities scrambling to understand the sheer scale of its operations.

Law enforcement agencies across the globe began sounding the alarm. Governments realized that AlphaBay was not just another dark web marketplace—it was the **largest criminal marketplace the internet had ever seen**. The problem was that, unlike traditional criminal organizations, AlphaBay had no physical headquarters, no central warehouse, and no easy point of entry for law enforcement to exploit. Its servers were scattered across multiple countries, its transactions hidden behind layers of encryption, and its administrators masked by false identities.

Authorities knew they had to act. But tracking a marketplace like AlphaBay was unlike any investigation they had ever undertaken. The **traditional methods of police work—wiretaps, undercover agents, forensic accounting—were ineffective** in a world where transactions were conducted in cryptocurrency, where no physical evidence changed hands, and where criminals never met in person.

Instead, they had to rely on **digital forensics, cyber-intelligence, and international cooperation**. Intelligence agencies in the United States, Europe, and Asia pooled their resources, attempting to map

AlphaBay's network and identify its key players. Every transaction, every user review, every leaked piece of data was analyzed for clues that could provide a way in. But for all their efforts, AlphaBay remained untouchable.

Part of its resilience came from its adaptability. Cazes, its creator, was not just running a marketplace—he was constantly improving it. He introduced **multi-layered security protocols**, including two-factor authentication, encrypted communications, and **Monero**, a cryptocurrency even more anonymous than Bitcoin. He **responded to law enforcement takedowns of smaller dark web markets by absorbing their users**, further consolidating AlphaBay's dominance.

What authorities found most concerning, however, was **who was using AlphaBay**. It was no longer just small-time drug dealers and identity thieves—it had become a **playground for international cartels, cyber-mercenaries, and state-sponsored hackers**.

The most powerful criminal organizations in the world saw the dark web as an opportunity. Mexican and Colombian cartels **moved high-purity drugs across borders** without ever stepping foot in another country. Eastern European cybercrime syndicates **sold stolen data in bulk, targeting major financial institutions** and corporations. **Hackers-for-hire offered espionage services**, infiltrating corporate networks and even government agencies. Some intelligence analysts suspected that **nation-states were using dark web markets like AlphaBay to conduct covert operations**, paying hackers in cryptocurrency to disrupt their geopolitical rivals.

The scale of it all was **unprecedented**. And yet, despite its power, AlphaBay was not invincible. For all its security measures, all its encrypted layers, and all its anonymized transactions, there was still a weakness. A flaw so small, so seemingly insignificant, that even Cazes himself did not recognize it.

And that flaw was about to bring the empire crashing down.

CHAPTER 5

The Hunt Begins—Law Enforcement Takes Notice

For years, AlphaBay operated with impunity, growing into an empire that law enforcement agencies around the world could no longer ignore. The sheer scale of its operations, the billions of dollars in illicit transactions, and the global reach of its vendors had transformed it from a mere dark web marketplace into the largest criminal economy ever seen online. Governments were no longer dealing with small-time hackers or isolated drug dealers—they were facing a fully functional, **decentralized black market**, run with the precision of a multinational corporation.

At first, law enforcement could do little but watch. AlphaBay had been designed with security in mind, ensuring that users remained anonymous and transactions were difficult to trace. Traditional investigative methods were useless in an environment where real names were never used, addresses were encrypted, and purchases were made with untraceable cryptocurrency. Surveillance cameras, wiretaps, and undercover informants—the standard tools of law enforcement—had no place in a world where crime was committed entirely in the digital sphere.

But the marketplace's success was also its greatest vulnerability. The larger it grew, the harder it became to remain invisible. Law enforcement agencies, intelligence units, and cybersecurity teams around the world began pooling their resources, forming **international task forces dedicated specifically to tracking AlphaBay and similar dark web platforms**. The FBI, the Drug Enforcement Administration (DEA), Europol, and numerous other agencies launched full-scale investigations, determined to map out the network and identify those who ran it.

Tracking AlphaBay's activity was no easy task. Unlike traditional online marketplaces that operated within regulated frameworks, AlphaBay existed in a **shadow economy**, hidden behind layers of encryption and designed to evade detection. But while individual transactions were difficult to trace, the sheer volume of traffic moving through the platform provided investigators with valuable data points. Every review left by a buyer, every transaction recorded on the blockchain, and every vendor listing created a **pattern**, and those patterns became the starting point for a deeper investigation.

Authorities had learned from their previous takedowns of Silk Road and other dark web markets. They knew that finding AlphaBay's users would be nearly impossible, but **the marketplace itself had to**

be hosted somewhere, and its administrators—no matter how careful—had to make mistakes eventually. Every criminal operation, no matter how sophisticated, left behind traces of human error. And in AlphaBay's case, those errors came from none other than its own creator.

For all his skill in cybersecurity and operational security, Alexandre Cazes had one fatal flaw—**he underestimated law enforcement's ability to connect the dots**. While he had taken extensive precautions to keep AlphaBay secure, he made small, seemingly insignificant mistakes that would eventually unravel everything.

One of those mistakes was his **digital footprint**. Unlike true ghosts in the cyber world, Cazes had a past—a past that included **reusing usernames, email accounts, and even passwords across different platforms**. His online alias, **Alpha02**, had been linked to hacking forums and underground communities long before AlphaBay was created. Investigators searching for connections between the administrator of AlphaBay and other known cybercriminals **began noticing patterns in his activity**, identifying posts and credentials that pointed to the same individual.

Another mistake was his **failure to separate his personal and criminal operations completely**. Cazes, despite his expertise in hiding digital transactions, made **careless financial decisions** that put him on law enforcement's radar. While his marketplace was designed for anonymity, **his lavish lifestyle was not**. Authorities began tracking **luxury assets purchased with cryptocurrency**, identifying properties, exotic cars, and expensive travel patterns that didn't match any known legitimate income sources. His purchase history began **painting a picture of someone with immense, unexplained wealth**.

The first real break in the investigation came when law enforcement **identified one of AlphaBay's servers**. While Cazes had taken precautions to distribute the infrastructure across multiple locations, a misconfiguration in one of the hosting services provided investigators with a lead—**a critical vulnerability that allowed them to monitor some of the platform's activity in real time**.

From there, they began **infiltrating AlphaBay's network**. Undercover agents posing as buyers and sellers created accounts, interacting with vendors and documenting their findings. They studied **the flow of transactions**, identifying key players and watching as millions of dollars in Bitcoin and Monero exchanged hands.

Each interaction provided more evidence. Each transaction created another data point. And while AlphaBay's vendors and buyers believed they were operating in complete secrecy, **law enforcement was slowly piecing together the puzzle**.

Cazes himself **was becoming reckless**. As AlphaBay continued to thrive, he **became more visible**, leaving behind subtle but crucial clues that allowed authorities to tighten their net. He wasn't just running a criminal empire—he was flaunting it.

The hunt was no longer just about bringing down a marketplace. It was about bringing down the man who believed he was untouchable. And the noose was tightening.

CHAPTER 6

AlphaBay's Fatal Mistakes

For all the layers of encryption, all the sophisticated security measures, and all the precautions taken to ensure AlphaBay remained untouchable, its downfall did not come from a cutting-edge law enforcement breakthrough. It was not a groundbreaking new surveillance technique or a high-tech digital forensics tool that led to its unraveling. Instead, it was something far simpler—human error.

Alexandre Cazes had built AlphaBay to be an impenetrable fortress, a place where criminals could operate without fear of detection. But despite his meticulous efforts to secure the marketplace, he overlooked one of the most basic principles of anonymity: **the past never truly disappears**. Long before he became the mastermind behind the largest dark web marketplace in history, Cazes had made seemingly minor mistakes that, years later, would come back to haunt him.

The first and most crucial misstep was **his old Hotmail account**. Investigators searching for leads on AlphaBay's origins stumbled upon something unexpected—an email address that had been used to send out welcome messages to new users when the site first launched. It was an amateur mistake, one that went against everything Cazes should have known about operational security. That email address—linked to an old, personal Hotmail account—provided investigators with a **direct connection between AlphaBay's administration and a real-world identity**.

It was a crack in the armor, and once law enforcement had it, they began pulling at the threads.

Cazes had used the same email in earlier online activities, registering on hacking forums, signing up for services, and leaving traces of his presence across multiple platforms. Each instance was a **breadcrumb leading back to him**, revealing a pattern of behavior that made it easier for investigators to confirm his identity.

But that wasn't his only mistake. Like many who believe themselves untouchable, **Cazes had a habit of reusing digital identities and passwords**. He operated across multiple underground forums, using variations of the same username—**Alpha02**—long before AlphaBay was created. Investigators, now focused on mapping his online activity, began connecting his forum posts, IP logs, and transaction histories. Every reused alias, every repeated password, every familiar writing style painted a clearer picture of the man behind AlphaBay.

Even with these connections, catching Cazes would still have been difficult if not for the **single most devastating mistake of all**—his laptop.

When law enforcement finally closed in, they needed undeniable proof that Cazes was not just affiliated with AlphaBay but that he was its administrator. The perfect scenario, one that would leave no room for denial, was to catch him with evidence in real time. And that is exactly what happened.

On the day of his arrest, **his laptop was open, unlocked, and logged into AlphaBay as an administrator**. It was a critical error, one that sealed his fate instantly. Had he been able to encrypt the device or shut it down before authorities reached him, the case might have been harder to prove. But with the laptop in an active session, investigators gained **immediate access to AlphaBay's internal systems**, including transaction records, messages between vendors and buyers, and administrator-level controls.

The laptop held **unquestionable evidence**—private encryption keys, financial ledgers, communications with AlphaBay staff, and even files linking him directly to his dark web empire. It was an open confession in digital form, an admission of guilt that required no interrogation, no forced confessions, no speculation.

With this information, the international effort to dismantle AlphaBay accelerated. The **FBI, Europol, and law enforcement agencies from multiple countries worked in coordination**, moving swiftly to shut down the marketplace's servers, seize its cryptocurrency holdings, and cut off access for its users. They tracked financial transactions, identified vendors, and began issuing warrants for those involved in its operations.

Cazes had believed that AlphaBay was bulletproof. But in the end, it was his own **digital footprints**—scattered across years of online activity—that led directly to his downfall. His past, his habits, and his overconfidence had all converged in a perfect storm, leaving behind a trail so obvious that even the most advanced encryption in the world couldn't protect him.

The most powerful dark web marketplace in history had finally met its match, not because of superior technology, but because of the **very human mistakes of the man who built it**.

CHAPTER 7

The Takedown—How Law Enforcement Shut Down AlphaBay

The takedown of AlphaBay was unlike any cybercrime operation the world had seen before. It was not a simple shutdown, nor was it the work of a single agency. It was a **global strike**, meticulously coordinated among the **FBI, DEA, Europol, Thai authorities**, and law enforcement agencies from multiple countries. AlphaBay had become too big to ignore, too dangerous to let operate any longer. The billions of dollars flowing through its encrypted channels were not just fueling underground crime— they were **empowering drug cartels, cybercriminal** syndicates, and fraud rings operating on a global scale.

But bringing down a marketplace as vast and sophisticated as AlphaBay required **more than just brute force**. This was not a street bust. There were no warehouses to raid, no drug stashes to seize, no physical evidence to collect. AlphaBay was **a digital empire**, spread across multiple encrypted servers in different countries, protected by layers of anonymization, and run by users who rarely revealed their real identities.

So law enforcement did not just aim to shut it down. **They wanted to own it first.**

The Operation Begins

The first step in dismantling AlphaBay was identifying its **infrastructure**. Unlike Silk Road, which was taken down after the arrest of its founder, AlphaBay's network was **distributed across**

multiple servers, designed to withstand government attacks. But through painstaking cyber-investigation, authorities located key servers running the marketplace. The breakthrough came when **one of the servers was discovered in the Netherlands**, its encryption misconfigured in a way that allowed law enforcement to **monitor a portion of AlphaBay's operations**. This was the window they had been waiting for.

Simultaneously, authorities **tracked Alexandre Cazes**, who had unknowingly left behind a digital breadcrumb trail. His lavish lifestyle in Thailand—**a fleet of luxury cars, multimillion-dollar homes, and high-profile financial transactions**—had caught the attention of Thai authorities. Cazes was living far beyond the means of any legal occupation, and investigators began **building a financial case against him**, tracking **cryptocurrency transactions that linked his personal wealth to AlphaBay's profits**.

But even with the pieces coming together, law enforcement still needed **one crucial element**—an opportunity to catch Cazes **while he was actively logged into AlphaBay.**

The Perfect Moment: Cazes' Arrest

On **July 5, 2017**, authorities moved in. Thai police, acting on intelligence from the **FBI and Europol**, raided Cazes' home in Bangkok. Timing was everything. They knew if he sensed danger, he could **encrypt his laptop in seconds**, locking away the evidence forever. But they were faster. When officers stormed his residence, Cazes' **laptop was open, unlocked, and logged in as AlphaBay's administrator.**

It was **the ultimate mistake**, the **holy grail of digital evidence.**

From that moment, AlphaBay was no longer a mystery. **Authorities now had full access to the**

marketplace's internal operations, including its financial records, user communications, and administrative controls. It was no longer a faceless, untraceable entity. It was an open book, a detailed record of years of illegal transactions, laid bare before the law.

But shutting it down immediately **was not the plan**. Instead, authorities executed one of the most sophisticated cyber-psychological operations in history.

Hijacking AlphaBay Before the Shutdown

Rather than immediately pulling the plug, law enforcement decided to **keep AlphaBay online, secretly hijacking its operations**. The goal was **to lure vendors, buyers, and other criminals into exposing themselves** before they had a chance to flee to alternative dark web markets.

For **two full weeks**, AlphaBay **appeared operational**, while in reality, it was under full government control. Law enforcement monitored user activity, gathering as much intelligence as possible. **Emails, transactions, and private messages** were logged. Those who continued conducting business on the platform unknowingly fed authorities **incriminating evidence**, which would later lead to multiple arrests and the tracking of illicit funds.

Then, without warning, **AlphaBay vanished.**

On **July 13, 2017**, the site **was taken offline permanently**. To the public, it looked like an **exit scam**—a common occurrence in dark web markets, where administrators disappear with users' funds. But within hours, the truth began to surface. **This was no exit scam. This was a full-scale law enforcement takedown.**

Seizing AlphaBay's Servers and Assets

As the site disappeared, a coordinated wave of **server seizures** unfolded across multiple countries. The Netherlands, Canada, and the United States were among the key locations where AlphaBay's infrastructure was housed. Investigators **froze cryptocurrency wallets** linked to AlphaBay, effectively locking away **millions of dollars in illicit funds** before vendors and buyers could withdraw their assets.

But the operation did not end with the takedown. **Law enforcement had AlphaBay's entire database.** They had **years of transaction records, thousands of user accounts, and financial trails leading to real-world criminals.** Over the next few months, authorities launched targeted arrests, tracking down **high-profile vendors and major fraudsters** who had once believed they were beyond the reach of the law.

The End of AlphaBay—Or Just the Beginning?

AlphaBay was gone. The largest illicit marketplace in internet history had been **infiltrated, hijacked, and dismantled**. The takedown was hailed as **one of the most significant victories against cybercrime**, proving that **no dark web market, no matter how sophisticated, was truly untouchable**.

But in the world of cybercrime, **a void never stays empty for long**. Even as authorities celebrated AlphaBay's fall, **new markets were already emerging**, learning from its mistakes, evolving to be even more elusive.

The game was not over. It had simply entered its next phase.

CHAPTER 8

The Arrest of Alexandre Cazes

For years, Alexandre Cazes had lived a life of unimaginable luxury, hidden in plain sight. While his digital empire thrived in the shadows of the dark web, his personal life was anything but discreet. He drove **Lamborghinis, owned multi-million-dollar homes, and had a financial portfolio that rivaled legitimate business tycoons**. From his luxurious villa in Bangkok, he controlled AlphaBay's sprawling network, moving millions of dollars in cryptocurrency with the ease of a Wall Street financier.

But what Cazes failed to realize was that his extravagance was also his downfall. **Criminal**

anonymity requires discipline—a complete disconnection between illegal operations and personal identity. Yet, despite all of his cybersecurity expertise, he made one fatal mistake: **he allowed his wealth to become visible**.

Tracking Cazes to His Bangkok Hideout

Authorities had been watching him long before they moved in. His real-world assets—**exotic cars, property investments, and sudden influxes of money into offshore accounts**—had drawn suspicion. No known legitimate business could justify the level of wealth he was accumulating, and financial crime units flagged his accounts for further scrutiny.

By the time law enforcement had linked Cazes to AlphaBay, they already had an idea of his physical location. **Thai authorities, working closely with the FBI and Europol, traced him to his home in an upscale neighborhood in Bangkok**. The house, a sprawling modern villa, was equipped with state-of-the-art security. Cazes lived like a man who had everything—because, in his mind, he had outsmarted the system.

He had grown so confident in his ability to remain hidden that he **stopped looking over his shoulder**. But on **July 5, 2017**, the illusion of invincibility shattered.

The Arrest: A Race Against Time

The timing of the operation was everything. Investigators **needed to catch Cazes with his laptop open and logged into AlphaBay**—a crucial piece of evidence that would tie him directly to the operation. If he had **even a few seconds of warning**, he could have encrypted his files, locked his accounts, and erased crucial evidence, making it far more difficult to prosecute him.

Thai police launched a **coordinated dawn raid**, storming his home before he had a chance to react.

The moment they entered, **Cazes was at his laptop, logged in as the AlphaBay administrator**. In that instant, his world collapsed. The authorities had the proof they needed—not just of his involvement, but of his control over the largest dark web marketplace in history.

The luxury cars in his garage, the bank records, the high-end watches—it was all **paid for with the proceeds of crime**, and now, there was no way to deny it.

The Interrogation: What Did Cazes Reveal?

Cazes was taken into custody at **Narcotics Suppression Bureau headquarters in Bangkok**. Officials from multiple countries were eager to question him. He was a **gold mine of information**—the architect of a billion-dollar criminal enterprise. Law enforcement wanted to know **everything**:

- How AlphaBay was structured
- Where the servers were located
- Who the top vendors were
- How funds were moved and laundered

But Cazes did not immediately cooperate. He was **calm, composed, and confident**, believing that **his legal team could negotiate his release**. After all, he was in Thailand—not in the direct custody of the United States. **He assumed that, at worst, he would be extradited and have time to prepare a legal defense**.

Yet, as the hours passed, it became clear that the case against him was airtight. **The evidence on his laptop alone was overwhelming**—transaction histories, communication logs, access credentials. He had been caught **red-handed**, and he knew it.

The Suspicious Circumstances of His Death

Then, **just seven days later**, everything took a shocking turn.

On **July 12, 2017**, while awaiting extradition to the United States, Cazes was found dead in his jail cell. Official reports stated that he had **hanged himself using a towel in his prison bathroom**. Thai authorities ruled it a **suicide**, a claim that was immediately met with skepticism.

Cazes had been a **brilliant strategist**, someone who had built an entire empire on deception and control. **Why would a man who had spent years outmaneuvering law enforcement suddenly decide to take his own life—before even facing trial?**

Theories swirled in the aftermath of his death:

- **Did he kill himself to avoid extradition and a lifetime behind bars?**

- **Did someone silence him to prevent him from revealing critical information?**
- **Did law enforcement put pressure on him, leading to his sudden demise?**

Whatever the truth, one thing was undeniable—**with Cazes dead, AlphaBay had lost its leader, and the dark web had lost its most powerful marketplace**.

His empire had crumbled. His fortune was frozen. His secrets—exposed. The mastermind of the world's largest dark web marketplace was gone. But the ripple effects of his downfall were just beginning.

CHAPTER 9

The Aftermath—What Happened Next?

The fall of AlphaBay sent shockwaves across the dark web. In a single moment, the largest and most powerful illicit marketplace had vanished, leaving behind chaos, panic, and unanswered questions. The takedown was more than just the closure of a website—it was a **seismic event that upended the digital underworld**.

For years, AlphaBay had been the gold standard for criminals operating in the shadows, a place where transactions could be carried out with **confidence, security, and anonymity**. But now, its vendors and buyers were left exposed, unsure of whether they had simply lost access to their accounts—or if law enforcement was already tracing their steps.

The Ripple Effect Across the Dark Web

The immediate aftermath was **paranoia**.

AlphaBay's disappearance followed a pattern that many users recognized. Dark web marketplaces had shut down before, sometimes due to law enforcement action, but other times because administrators **orchestrated exit scams**, vanishing with users' funds. In the first few days, many speculated that AlphaBay's creators had simply decided to cash out, pocketing the millions of dollars in escrowed funds and **leaving their users in the dark**.

But soon, the truth became undeniable. The coordinated arrests, the **international operation led by the FBI, DEA, Europol, and Thai police**, and the official announcement from law enforcement confirmed that **AlphaBay hadn't disappeared—it had been taken down**.

The moment it became clear that **governments had infiltrated and seized AlphaBay's servers**, fear spread like wildfire. Vendors **frantically erased their digital footprints**, deleting accounts, shutting down operations, and warning their customers to **stay low**. Buyers scrambled to withdraw cryptocurrency holdings, while others **disappeared from the dark web entirely**, fearing that their transaction histories were now in the hands of investigators.

The closure of AlphaBay also **disrupted the global supply chain of illicit goods**, particularly in the drug trade. Vendors who relied on the marketplace **lost their primary sales channel**, forcing them to either **relocate to smaller markets** or risk returning to street-level distribution. For some, the loss of AlphaBay meant financial ruin. For others, it was simply a temporary setback—an opportunity to migrate to the next big platform.

The Rise of New Marketplaces

In the underworld, **demand never disappears**—it only shifts. Within weeks of AlphaBay's shutdown, new marketplaces emerged to take its place. Among them, **Dream Market** and **Empire Market** became the largest successors, absorbing much of AlphaBay's displaced user base.

Dream Market, which had already been operational for years, experienced a **massive surge in activity**, as both vendors and buyers flooded its servers. But it was **Empire Market**, launched in the aftermath of AlphaBay's fall, that sought to position itself as the new dominant player. **It implemented many of the same security features that had made AlphaBay successful**, including multi-signature escrow, encrypted communications, and Monero transactions for added anonymity.

But these markets were operating **under a new level of scrutiny**. Law enforcement agencies had proven that they could infiltrate and dismantle even the most **sophisticated dark web operations**, and marketplace administrators knew that they were now being watched more closely than ever before. This **led to an era of heightened security measures**, with newer markets adopting **advanced encryption, stricter vendor verification, and even requiring buyers to prove their trustworthiness before gaining access to high-level sellers**.

However, the rapid rise and fall of dark web markets had now become **the new norm**. AlphaBay's demise showed that **no platform was safe**, and **trust in the dark web economy was permanently shaken**.

How Law Enforcement Used AlphaBay's Data to Track Criminals

While vendors and buyers were scrambling to find new platforms, **law enforcement was just getting started**.

The **seizure of AlphaBay's servers was a goldmine**. Investigators now had access to **transaction records, communication logs, and the identities of thousands of vendors and customers**. Even though these individuals had taken precautions to remain anonymous, **mistakes had been made**—email addresses, cryptocurrency transactions, and delivery addresses left trails that could be followed.

Authorities launched **waves of arrests**, targeting some of AlphaBay's **largest vendors**. Individuals who had moved millions of dollars' worth of illicit goods suddenly found themselves facing federal indictments. In the months and years that followed, **dozens of high-profile dark web dealers were**

arrested, their identities unmasked by forensic analysis of AlphaBay's transaction history.

One of the biggest breakthroughs came from **tracing cryptocurrency transactions**. Even though **Bitcoin and Monero** were used to anonymize payments, law enforcement had **developed new blockchain analysis tools** that allowed them to **deanonymize certain transactions**, exposing the individuals behind them.

In some cases, **AlphaBay users had linked their cryptocurrency wallets to real-world exchanges**, allowing authorities to connect illicit transactions to **real identities**. Others had used **weak operational security (OPSEC)**, repeating usernames, emails, or other identifiers across different platforms—just as Cazes had done.

This was a warning to the entire dark web: **Even if you weren't caught today, the data from**

AlphaBay could still come back to haunt you years later.

The Ongoing Battle Between Cybercriminals and Law Enforcement

The takedown of AlphaBay marked a **turning point** in the war between cybercriminals and law enforcement. It proved that, despite the dark web's promise of **anonymity and decentralization,** governments were **capable of infiltrating, dismantling, and tracking even the most sophisticated black markets.**

However, it also highlighted a **harsh reality:** **demand for illicit goods and services would never disappear. As long as there were buyers, there would always be sellers.** And as long as there were sellers, there would always be new platforms rising from the ashes of those that fell.

The dark web was evolving. In response to AlphaBay's takedown, **newer markets became more decentralized, implementing stronger encryption, and shifting towards even more privacy-focused cryptocurrencies** like **Zcash and Monero**, which were designed to be even harder to trace than Bitcoin.

Meanwhile, law enforcement agencies continued **developing new forensic tools**, investing in **AI-driven blockchain analysis**, cyber-infiltration techniques, and undercover digital operations. They knew that **new markets would rise**—but they were now **better prepared than ever** to hunt them down.

AlphaBay's fall was not the end of the dark web's illicit economy. **It was the beginning of a new chapter—one where the battle between cybercriminals and authorities would never truly end.**

CHAPTER 10

The Evolution of Cybercrime

The takedown of AlphaBay was a historic moment in the battle against cybercrime, proving that even the most sophisticated dark web marketplace was not immune to law enforcement. But in the ever-evolving world of digital crime, no single victory is permanent. **AlphaBay's fall was not the end of dark web commerce—it was merely a shift in the landscape.**

Just as Silk Road's demise gave rise to AlphaBay, the closure of AlphaBay led to a new generation of cybercriminals, marketplaces, and technological advancements designed to stay ahead of law enforcement. If anything, the fall of the dark web's largest black market only served as a **lesson for those who would come next**.

The Evolution of Dark Web Crime

The demand for illicit goods and services never disappeared—it simply **moved to new platforms, adopting more advanced security measures**. In the wake of AlphaBay's collapse, cybercriminals learned from the mistakes of their predecessors. New dark web marketplaces began incorporating **stronger encryption, more decentralized hosting structures, and even more anonymous cryptocurrencies** to avoid detection.

One of the biggest changes was the move away from Bitcoin as the **primary currency of cybercrime**. While Bitcoin had once been considered untraceable, forensic analysis tools developed by law enforcement agencies began **deanonymizing transactions**, allowing authorities to track criminal activity through blockchain records. This led to the rise of **Monero,**

Zcash, and other privacy-focused cryptocurrencies, which offered even stronger transactional secrecy.

Modern cybercriminals also shifted their communications to **encrypted messaging apps and private forums**. Open dark web forums, which had once been hubs for illicit trade, became **too risky**, as law enforcement continued to infiltrate and monitor them. Instead, criminals turned to **invite-only Telegram groups, Discord servers, and decentralized messaging platforms** that provided stronger security against infiltration.

The Rise of Decentralized Dark Web Markets

While early dark web markets were often controlled by **centralized administrators**, AlphaBay's fall made criminals rethink this structure. A single point of failure—a leader like Cazes, who could be identified and arrested—was too risky.

This led to the emergence of **decentralized dark web marketplaces**, which used blockchain-based smart contracts, peer-to-peer networks, and distributed hosting to prevent a single point of failure. Instead of relying on traditional escrow services controlled by a central administrator, these new platforms **allowed transactions to be settled autonomously through blockchain technology**, making them far harder to take down.

The Cat-and-Mouse Game Between Cybercriminals and Law Enforcement

Law enforcement agencies did not stop with AlphaBay. They adapted, learning from their success in taking down the platform. Governments **invested in AI-powered blockchain analysis, cyber-infiltration teams, and new regulations on cryptocurrency exchanges** to track and dismantle future marketplaces.

Dark web markets, in response, became **more fragmented**. Instead of one dominant platform like AlphaBay, cybercriminals **dispersed their activities across multiple smaller, more agile markets**, making large-scale takedowns more difficult.

One of the biggest battlegrounds in modern cybercrime is **privacy technology itself**. Governments worldwide are pushing for **stricter regulations on encrypted communications, cryptocurrencies, and anonymous browsing tools**, arguing that these technologies enable crime. But privacy advocates counter that such measures could **compromise civil liberties**, as these same tools are used by journalists, activists, and ordinary citizens who need protection from oppressive regimes.

Lessons Learned from AlphaBay's Rise and Fall

AlphaBay's story offers **a crucial lesson in the evolution of digital crime**—that no system is ever truly secure. While it was built with extreme precautions, its founder made mistakes that ultimately led to its downfall. **Personal greed, operational errors, and the inability to remain truly anonymous sealed Cazes' fate.**

But another lesson is just as important: **The war between cybercriminals and law enforcement is a never-ending cycle.** Every takedown leads to new innovations. Every innovation leads to new challenges. The fall of AlphaBay did not stop the underground economy; it merely forced it to evolve.

The Future of Online Crime and Cybersecurity

As cybercrime continues to evolve, so too does the fight against it. **Artificial intelligence, machine learning, and deep forensic analysis** are becoming powerful tools in identifying criminal activity online. But cybercriminals are just as quick to adapt, leveraging new technologies such as **AI-driven malware, quantum-resistant encryption, and** decentralized finance (DeFi) platforms to stay ahead.

The question remains: **Can law enforcement ever truly stop dark web crime?** Or will it continue to morph, shifting into new, even harder-to-trace forms?

The story of AlphaBay is a testament to both the **power and fragility of digital crime**. It built an empire, defied governments, and moved billions in illicit transactions. But in the end, **it fell just like the others before it**.

The dark web, however, remains. And the cycle continues.

CONCLUSION

The story of AlphaBay is not just about the rise and fall of a dark web marketplace—it is a defining chapter in the history of cybercrime. From its origins as a modest underground forum to its reign as the largest illicit market in digital history, AlphaBay reshaped the way crime was conducted online. It transformed the dark web from a fragmented collection of illegal traders into a **sophisticated, multi-billion-dollar economy**, where anonymity was the ultimate currency and law enforcement was just another obstacle to be bypassed.

Its collapse, however, sent a message that **no criminal empire, no matter how deeply embedded in the shadows, is truly untouchable**. The takedown of

AlphaBay was not just the dismantling of a website; it was the **largest coordinated cybercrime operation ever executed**, involving multiple governments, intelligence agencies, and forensic analysts working across borders. It was a **landmark victory** for law enforcement—proof that even in the digital underworld, mistakes can be exploited, identities can be unmasked, and power can be stripped away in an instant.

But as history has shown, **no single takedown is ever enough to end the dark web economy**. The disappearance of AlphaBay created **a power vacuum**, one that was quickly filled by new marketplaces, more resilient, more cautious, and more technologically advanced than their predecessors. In the wake of its fall, **cybercriminals learned from Cazes' mistakes**, developing **decentralized networks, encrypted payment systems, and more sophisticated operational security** to avoid the fate that had befallen AlphaBay.

Law enforcement, too, adapted. The techniques used to infiltrate and dismantle AlphaBay became **a blueprint for future cybercrime investigations**. Governments invested heavily in **AI-powered blockchain analysis, cyber-forensic tracking, and undercover infiltration**, determined to stay one step ahead of the criminals they pursued. Each new marketplace that rose in AlphaBay's place faced **greater scrutiny, greater risk, and greater resistance** from global authorities.

And yet, despite every shutdown, every arrest, and every hard-fought victory, the **dark web remains an ever-evolving battlefield**. The demand for illicit goods and services has not disappeared—it has merely changed form, shifting into new marketplaces, hidden messaging platforms, and decentralized digital networks designed to be even harder to police.

The battle between cybercriminals and law enforcement is a **game without an end**, a perpetual cycle of **innovation and counter-innovation, attack and defense, concealment and exposure**. The fall of AlphaBay was a turning point, but it was **not the conclusion of the story**. It was a reminder that in the digital world, **nothing is permanent, and no one is truly invisible**.

For every AlphaBay that falls, another will rise. And the chase will continue.